AI for Beginners — Kids Edition

Book 1: Introduction to AI

Created by
AI Circuit

ISBN: 978-1-970328-02-8
Printed in the United States of America
First Edition
AI Circuit
An imprint dedicated to kid-friendly STEM learning.

Dedicated to curious kids
everywhere.
Each page you turn brings you
closer
to understanding the world of
tomorrow.
— AI Circuit

SERIES NOTE

About This Series
AI for Beginners — Kids Edition is an 8-book learning adventure that makes Artificial Intelligence simple, friendly, and exciting for children.

Each volume focuses on one major part of AI—starting with the basics and growing into vision, language, robotics, ethics, and more.

This book, **Book 1: Introduction to AI**, gives readers a gentle, engaging first look at how smart systems learn and help people every day.

The Complete AI Adventure Series

Book 1 — Introduction to AI
Book 2 — Symbolic AI
Book 3 — Neural Networks
Book 4 — Computer Vision
Book 5 — Natural Language AI
Book 6 — Other AI Techniques
Book 7 — AI Ethics
Book 8 — Mega Activity Book

Each book opens the door to a new part of Artificial Intelligence—one kid-friendly concept at a time.

HOW TO USE THIS BOOK

This book is designed for:

- Curious kids ages 7–12
- Families learning together
- Teachers and homeschoolers
- STEM clubs and after-school programs

Each spread includes:

Story Narrative (Left Page)
A short scene that helps kids imagine how AI appears in their world.

and a

Concept Explanation
A clear, simple explanation of the idea from the story.

Illustration Prompt
The visual concept behind each picture.
Kids can read this book straight through or jump to any topic that sparks curiosity!

ACKNOWLEDGMENTS

Thank you to every teacher, parent, librarian, and homeschool family who believes in giving kids early access to big ideas.

Your support, encouragement, and passion for learning make books like this possible.

And to the young readers:
Your questions inspire every page we create.

ABOUT AI CIRCUIT

AI Circuit creates engaging, age-friendly books that make complex ideas—like coding, robotics, and artificial intelligence—simple, fun, and accessible.

We create books that help families, teachers, and 10-year-old explorers build confidence with future-ready skills

Our mission is to help kids build confidence with STEM and spark a lifelong curiosity for the technologies shaping their future.

★ GLOSSARY INTRODUCTION PAGE

Welcome to the AI Glossary!

Here you'll find simple explanations for some of the important words in this book.

These definitions make the stories easier to understand and help you learn how AI works.

But remember:
These are only a few words from a much bigger world of AI!

If you want to explore LOTS more kid-friendly AI terms, check out the **AI Children's Dictionary**, which has hundreds of fun, easy explanations.

Keep learning, keep exploring, and keep turning big ideas into simple ones!

Artificial Intelligence (AI)

Definition:
The field of computer science where machines are designed to learn, think, and make decisions.

In kid-friendly terms:
It's when computers act like smart helpers that can learn from examples.

Example:
A robot that learns to sort pictures of cats and dogs by studying thousands of images.

Imagine This Scene:
A friendly robot with glowing eyes looking at floating picture cards of animals, its mind lighting up as it recognizes patterns.

Concept

Definition:

An idea or category the AI learns internally.

In kid-friendly terms:

It's something the robot understands — like "**circle**," "**bird**," or "**happy**."

Example:

The AI forms a concept of "**bird**" by learning wings, feathers, and beaks go together.

Imagine This Scene:

A robot holding a glowing bubble labeled "**Bird Concept**," filled with tiny icons of wings, feathers, and beaks.

BIRD
CONCEPT

Concept Boundary

Definition:
The invisible border that separates one idea from another inside the AI's mind.

In kid-friendly terms:
It's the robot deciding what belongs in a category — and what doesn't.

Example:
Birds belong inside the "**bird**" concept boundary; bats do not.

Imagine This Scene:
A robot drawing a glowing circle around bird icons while gently pushing a bat icon outside.

Confidence Distribution

Definition:
How the AI spreads its confidence across all possible answers.

In kid-friendly terms:
It's the robot showing how much it believes in each guess.

Example:
For an animal picture:

- 60% cat
- 30% fox
- 10% raccoon

Imagine This Scene:
A robot examining multiple glowing bubbles of different sizes, each with a percentage inside.

92%
75%
60%
92%
31%
88%
31%
98%

Correction Signal

Definition:
A message that tells the AI how to adjust itself after a mistake.

In kid-friendly terms:
It's the robot being told, "**Try again—but fix it this way!**"

Example:
If the AI mistakes a wolf for a dog, the correction signal tells it to pay more attention to wolf features.

Imagine This Scene:
A glowing arrow labeled "**Try This Instead!**" points toward the right direction while the robot nods.

Data

Definition:
Information that an AI uses to learn, such as pictures, text, sounds, or numbers.

In kid-friendly terms:
It's everything the robot looks at to learn — like its homework.

Example:
A folder full of animal photos the AI studies to learn which animal is which.

Imagine This Scene:
A robot opening a glowing treasure chest filled with pictures, numbers, and icons swirling with sparkles.

Data Balance

Definition:
Having the same amount of examples for each category so the AI learns fairly.

In kid-friendly terms:
It's giving the robot equal practice with everything.

Example:
100 dog photos and 100 cat photos create a balanced dataset.

Imagine This Scene:
A robot weighing two glowing buckets — one full of cat photos and one full of dog photos — perfectly balanced.

Data Drift

Definition:
When the real-world data slowly changes over time, making old training examples less accurate.

In kid-friendly terms:
It's when the world changes, but the robot learned from old pictures.

Example:
An AI trained on summer plants struggles when winter snow covers them.

Imagine This Scene:
A robot comparing a glowing summer plant image with a snowy winter version, looking surprised.

Data Variety

Definition:
Having many different kinds of examples to help the AI learn better.

In kid-friendly terms:
It's giving the robot lots of different versions so it doesn't get confused.

Example:
Hundreds of pictures of cats — fluffy cats, black cats, kittens, sitting cats, running cats.

Imagine This Scene:
A robot surrounded by glowing cat pictures, all different shapes, sizes, and colors.

Decision Boundary

Definition:
An invisible line the AI uses to separate one category from another.

In kid-friendly terms:
It's the robot's rule for deciding: "**This goes here, that goes there.**"

Example:
A simple line separating "**cats**" from "**dogs**" based on their features.

Imagine This Scene:
A robot drawing a glowing line in the air between floating cat icons and dog icons.

Error / Mistake

Definition:
The difference between the AI's prediction and the correct answer.

In kid-friendly terms:
It's when the robot gets something wrong.

Example:
The AI looks at a fox and predicts "**dog.**"
That's an error.

Imagine This Scene:
A robot showing a glowing "**WRONG!**" bubble, then looking embarrassed as the right answer appears beside it.

?
WRONG!

Error Reduction Step

Definition:
A tiny improvement the AI makes to reduce its mistakes during training.

In kid-friendly terms:
It's the robot fixing its errors one little step at a time.

Example:
If the AI keeps confusing zebras and horses, each tiny adjustment helps it get a little better at telling them apart.

Imagine This Scene:
A robot dropping tiny glowing “er**ror pebbles**” off a magic scale, making one side slowly rise as mistakes disappear.

Feature

Definition:
A specific clue or detail in the data that helps the AI make a decision.

In kid-friendly terms:
It's the hint the robot uses — like stripes, shapes, colors, or sounds.

Example:
For a cat, useful features include whiskers, pointy ears, and a tail.

Imagine This Scene:
A robot highlighting glowing feature icons —ears, whiskers, tail—around a cat picture.

Feature Interaction

Definition:
When two or more clues work together to help the AI make a better prediction.

In kid-friendly terms:
It's when hints team up to give the robot a stronger answer.

Example:
To identify a tiger, the AI uses stripes + sharp teeth together.

Imagine This Scene:
A robot holding two glowing feature icons that magically combine into a brighter, more powerful clue.

Feature Robustness

Definition:
How useful a clue remains even when the input changes or gets messy.

In kid-friendly terms:
It's a hint the robot can always rely on, even when pictures get weird.

Example:
A giraffe's long neck is a strong, reliable feature—even in shadows or strange angles.

Imagine This Scene:
A robot testing a glowing "**long neck**" feature under different lighting and shapes, and it stays bright.

Feature Strength

Definition:
How important or powerful a clue is for helping the AI make a decision.

In kid-friendly terms:
It's how loudly a clue "**speaks**" to the robot.

Example:
When spotting birds, "**feathers**" may have much stronger feature strength than "**color**."

Imagine This Scene:
A robot comparing glowing feature bubbles — one big and bright (important), one tiny and dim (less important).

Good Data

Definition:
Clear, correct, and helpful information that makes it easier for AI to learn.

In kid-friendly terms:
It's the best kind of "**homework**" for the robot — clean, fair, and easy to understand.

Example:
Bright, labeled pictures of animals help AI learn their differences correctly.

Imagine This Scene:
A happy robot studying a glowing shelf of clear, colorful pictures while sparkles float around the neat examples.

Input

Definition:
The information you give to the AI so it can make a prediction.

In kid-friendly terms:
It's what the robot looks at or listens to before answering.

Example:
Showing the AI a picture of a dog and asking, "*What is this*?"

Imagine This Scene:
A robot staring at a glowing picture frame being handed to it, ready to make a guess.

Input Ambiguity

Definition:
When an input can be understood in more than one way.

In kid-friendly terms:
It's when the robot says, "*Hmm... this could be TWO things!*"

Example:
A shadowy figure might look like either a fluffy sheep or a cloud.

Imagine This Scene:
A robot staring at a blurry glowing image while two guess bubbles ("sheep?" and "cloud?") float beside it.

GUESS: CLOUD?
GUESS: SHEEP?

Input Quality

Definition:
How clear, complete, and useful the input is for the AI.

In kid-friendly terms:
It's how "**nice and clean**" the robot's clues are.

Example:
A clear, bright photo helps the AI predict correctly. A blurry, dark one makes it harder.

Imagine This Scene:
A robot comparing a glowing sharp image next to a fuzzy dim one, choosing the clearer one.

Input Variation

Definition:
All the different ways the same thing can appear to the AI.

In kid-friendly terms:
It's how the robot sees the same thing in many different forms.

Example:
A chair seen from the side, from above, close-up, far away, or in different lighting.

Imagine This Scene:
A robot surrounded by glowing versions of the same chair image—different angles, colors, sizes.

Label

Definition:

The correct answer that tells the AI what each example is.

In kid-friendly terms:

It's the name tag that teaches the robot the right answer.

Example:

A photo of a dog with the word "**DOG**" beneath it helps the AI learn what dogs look like.

Imagine This Scene:

A robot holding a glowing tag labeled "**PUPPY**" and placing it under a dog picture.

PUPPY

Learning

Definition:
The process where AI improves its ability to recognize patterns and make decisions by studying examples.

In kid-friendly terms:
It's the robot practicing until it gets better and better.

Example:
The AI looks at thousands of photos of birds and learns to recognize them on its own.

Imagine This Scene:
A robot reading glowing picture cards in a loop — with each loop it gets a little brighter and more confident.

Learning Rate

Definition:
A number that controls how big each learning step is during training.

In kid-friendly terms:
It tells the robot whether to learn with tiny steps or giant leaps.

Example:
A big learning rate may make the robot jump too far.
A small learning rate makes it learn slowly but safely.

Imagine This Scene:
A robot adjusting a glowing dial labeled "**Small Steps → Big Steps**," surrounded by sparkly motion trails.

Small Steps
Big Steps

Loss

Definition:
A number that tells the AI how wrong its prediction was.

In kid-friendly terms:
It's the robot's "**how wrong was I?**" score.

Example:
Guessing "**cat**" when the answer is "**tiger**" gives a big loss.
Guessing "cat" when the answer is "**cat**" gives a tiny loss.

Imagine This Scene:
A robot comparing a tall glowing red loss bar (big mistake) and a tiny green bar (small mistake).

LOSSES
GAINS

Model (AI Model)

Definition:
A trained system that can make predictions or decisions based on what it has learned.

In kid-friendly terms:
It's the robot's "**brain**" after it finishes learning from examples.

Example:
After training on animal photos, the model can guess the animal in a new picture.

Imagine This Scene:
A robot glowing "**brain crystal**" that lights up whenever it makes a prediction.

Noise

Definition:
Unwanted or messy information that makes it hard for the AI to understand the input.

In kid-friendly terms:
It's the robot trying to see a picture through scribbles or static.

Example:
A blurry or shadowy animal photo filled with distractions.

Imagine This Scene:
A robot brushing away glowing static sparkles covering an image, trying to reveal the clear picture.

Noise Sensitivity

Definition:
How easily the AI gets confused by messy or distorted data.

In kid-friendly terms:
It's how much noisy pictures bother the robot.

Example:
A sensitive AI struggles with even a small blur; a strong AI handles more noise easily.

Imagine This Scene:
A nervous robot examining a noisy blurry image while a confident robot stands strong beside a clearer one.

Optimization

Definition:
The process of making the AI better by reducing its mistakes over time.

In kid-friendly terms:
It's the robot's mission to keep getting smarter.

Example:
Each training cycle helps the AI get more accurate at spotting animals.

Imagine This Scene:
A robot tuning glowing dials and switches on its "**learning panel**," with sparkles bursting as it improves.

Output

Definition:
The answer or prediction the AI gives after analyzing the input.

In kid-friendly terms:
It's the robot's final answer.

Example:
The AI looks at a photo and says, "*This is a tree*."

Imagine This Scene:
A robot pointing to a floating glowing answer bubble labeled "**TREE!**" with excitement.

Pattern Recognition

Definition:
The ability of AI to find similarities, shapes, or repeated structures in data.

In kid-friendly terms:
It's the robot noticing things that look alike — like stripes, shapes, or sounds.

Example:
The AI sees stripes on many animals and learns "**stripes often mean tiger or zebra**."

Imagine This Scene:
A robot pointing to bright glowing patterns —dots, stripes, shapes—floating in the air, connecting them with sparkly lines.

Pattern Stability

Definition:
How steadily a pattern stays the same across different examples.

In kid-friendly terms:
It's when a clue keeps appearing again and again, even when things change a little.

Example:
Birds always have wings, whether they're big, small, flying, or resting.

Imagine This Scene:
A robot pointing to multiple glowing wing outlines that stay consistent across many animal images.

Pattern Strength

Definition:
How strongly the AI detects a certain pattern in the data.

In kid-friendly terms:
It's how loudly a pattern shouts, "*I'm here*!"

Example:
Bold zebra stripes create a strong, easy-to-recognize pattern.

Imagine This Scene:
A robot pointing to giant bright glowing stripe icons bursting with sparkles.

Prediction

Definition:
The answer an AI gives after analyzing the input.

In kid-friendly terms:
It's the robot's best guess.

Example:
The AI sees an image and says, "*I think this is a future city.*"

Imagine This Scene:
A robot holding up a glowing bubble that says "**FUTURE CITY!**" with a proud smile.

FUTURE FORECAST

Prediction Confidence

Definition:
A number showing how sure the AI is about its prediction.

In kid-friendly terms:
It's the robot saying, "*I'm really sure*!" or "*I'm only kinda sure.*"

Example:
The AI says it is 90% sure the picture shows a bird.

Imagine This Scene:
A robot pointing to a glowing confidence meter that rises from low to high.

CONFIDENCE

Predictive Stability

Definition:

When the AI gives the same correct answer even if the input changes slightly.

In kid-friendly terms:

It's the robot staying calm and correct, even when pictures get tricky.

Example:

The AI still says "chair" even if the photo gets a little darker.

Imagine This Scene:

A robot confidently showing the same glowing "**CHAIR!**" bubble while the image fades and brightens.

STEADY
ANSWER

Representation

Definition:
The way AI stores ideas, features, and patterns inside its "**idea space.**"

In kid-friendly terms:
It's the robot's secret map of how ideas connect.

Example:
Cats and lions are close together in the AI's idea space, but far from airplanes.

Imagine This Scene:
A robot floating in a magical glowing idea-galaxy with clusters of tiny icons grouped by similarity.

Sensors

Definition:
Tools that help robots notice the world, like tiny digital eyes, ears, and touchpads.

In kid-friendly terms:
It's how a robot "**sees,**" "**hears,**" "**feels,**" or senses things around it.

Example:
A robot uses light sensors to detect brightness and touch sensors to notice when someone taps it.

Imagine This Scene:
A little robot glows as tiny icons (eye, ear, hand) float around its crystal head, showing how it senses the world.

Training Cycle

Definition:
The full loop of learning: look at data → make a guess → see the answer → improve.

In kid-friendly terms:
It's the robot's practice routine: try, check, fix, try again.

Example:
An AI repeats hundreds of training cycles to learn to recognize fish.

Imagine This Scene:
A robot running in a glowing circular loop labeled **TRY → CHECK → FIX → TRY AGAIN.**

TRY
TRY
TRY
CHECK
T
FIX
TRY AGA
FIN

Training Data

Definition:
A special set of examples used to teach the AI how to make predictions.

In kid-friendly terms:
It's the robot's practice set — the examples it studies to learn.

Example:
Pictures of apples labeled "**apple**," oranges labeled "**orange**," and bananas labeled "**banana**."

Imagine This Scene:
A robot lined up in front of a glowing wall of labeled images with sparkly arrows pointing to each answer.

Uncertainty

Definition:
A measure of how unsure the AI is about its prediction.

In kid-friendly terms:
It's the robot saying, "*Hmm... I'm not sure about this one.*"

Example:
A blurry picture makes the AI unsure which one is correct.

Imagine This Scene:
A robot scratching its chin as two glowing guess-bubbles ("GUESS A?" "GUESS B?") float around.

GUESS A
?
GUESS B
31%

Underlying Pattern

Definition:
A hidden rule or structure in the data that the AI learns to recognize.

In kid-friendly terms:
It's the secret clue the robot discovers after seeing many examples.

Example:
The AI notices that animals with long ears and hopping movement are usually rabbits.

Imagine This Scene:
A robot shining a glowing flashlight onto picture cards, revealing sparkly patterns underneath.

STORY SPREADS

BEGIN HERE

What Is AI?

In science class, the ten-year-old kids gather around as their teacher lifts a glowing tablet. Strange icons swirl across the screen —robots, brains, lightning bolts, and little speech bubbles.

"*This*," the teacher says with a smile, "*is artificial intelligence.*"

Everyone leans closer, amazed to learn that smart machines are already around them every day.

Artificial Intelligence (AI) is when a computer is designed to act a little bit smart. It can learn patterns, make simple decisions, and help people do useful tasks.

When something feels like it can "**think**," even a tiny bit, you're probably looking at AI.

Everyday AI

On the bus ride home, Emma notices her phone suggests the fastest route.
At home, her brother asks a smart speaker to play music.
Their robot vacuum bumps gently around the living room.
"*Wow*," Emma whispers, "*AI is everywhere*!"

AI helps with everyday tasks: maps that find routes, speakers that follow voice commands, and machines that clean floors.

Many tools use AI quietly in the background—even if you don't notice it.

AI vs Human Thinking

During class, Emma asks, "*Does AI think like we do?*"

Her teacher smiles and shakes her head.

"*Humans understand feelings, ideas, and the world. AI notices patterns but doesn't truly 'think' like people.*"

Emma taps her chin. "*So robots don't feel excited or scared?*"

"*Nope,*" the teacher laughs. "*Only humans do that.*"

AI learns from examples and patterns, but it doesn't understand emotions or have real thoughts.

Humans can imagine, feel, dream, and understand meaning. AI can only do what it's trained to do.

HUMAN THINKING
AI THINKING

Machines That Learn

During homework time, Emma's tablet keeps getting better at guessing which math problems she needs help with.
"*It's like it's learning what I struggle with*," she thinks.

Some AI systems learn from examples. The more they practice, the better they get.
This is called machine learning—computers improving by studying patterns.

Patterns Everywhere

Noah watches birds outside and realizes they land on the same fence every morning.
"**That's a pattern**," he thinks.
His tablet suddenly shows a tip: "**Patterns help AI learn**!"

AI looks for patterns—things that happen again and again.

If it sees many examples, it can guess what might happen next.

AI Learns Slowly, Not Instantly

Noah asks, "*Can you learn chess in one second*?"
The robot shakes its head. "*Nope! I learn little by little.*"
Emma smiles. "*Just like us*!"

AI improves slowly, step by step — just like students do.

It practices many examples, fixes mistakes, and slowly gets better — step by step.

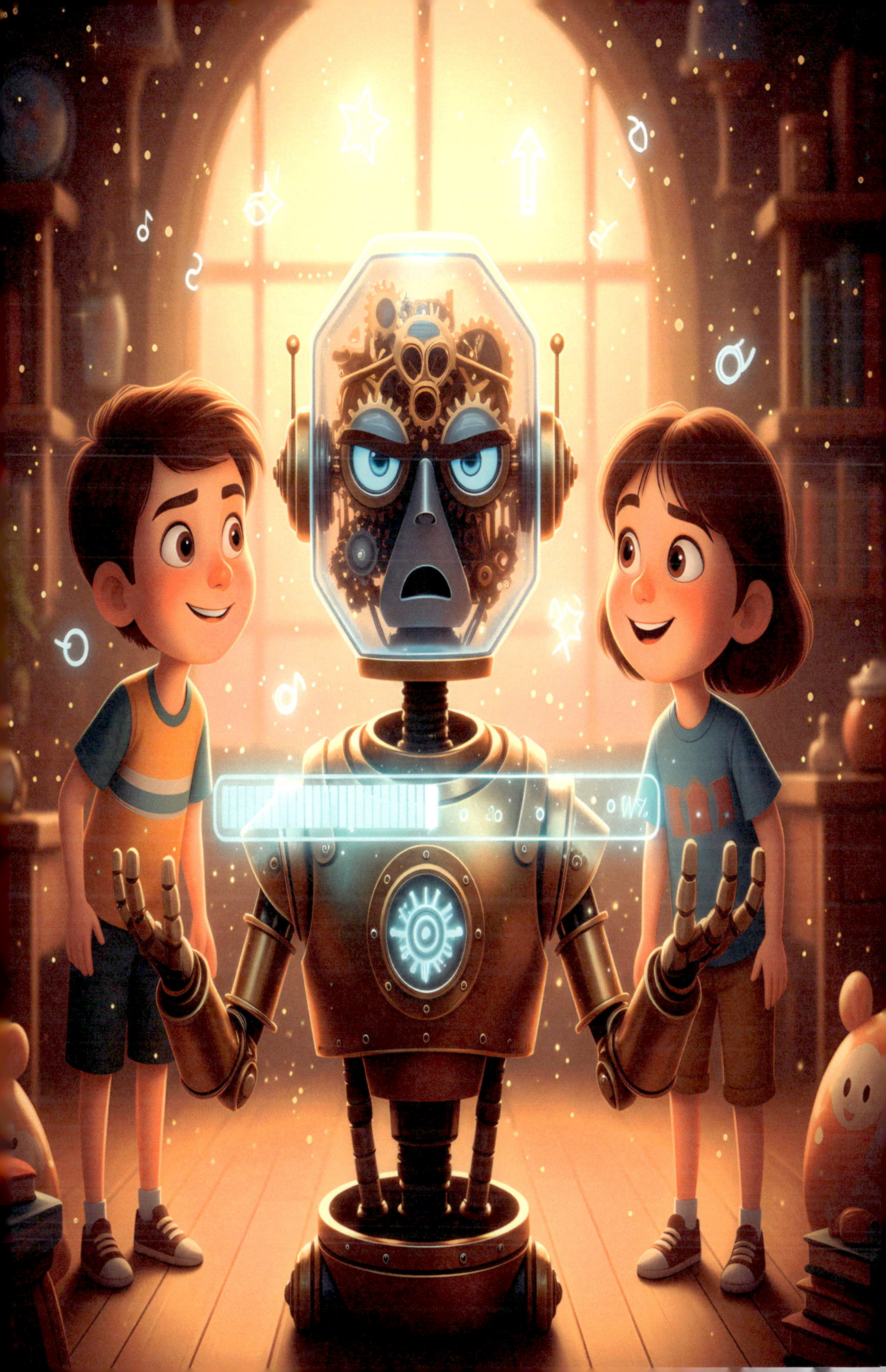

What Is Data?

During science club, Emma counts how many butterflies she sees each day.

"*Look at all your data*!" her teacher says.

Emma smiles—she didn't know she'd been collecting data all along.

Data is information: pictures, numbers, words, sounds, or anything you can record.

AI needs data to learn—just like 10-year-old kids need examples.

133496
1:2
6=3=
12:43

AI Works Best With Good Data

Emma gives her robot a blurry picture of a bird.
It guesses, "*Is this... a sandwich*?"
Emma laughs. "*No! You need better photos*!"

AI depends on the quality of its data.
Clear, balanced, correct examples help it learn.

Bad or messy data makes it confused.

Training AI

Emma uploads her butterfly photos into a learning app.

It asks, "*Is this a Monarch*? *Yes or no*?"

She answers again and again until the app starts guessing correctly on its own.

To train AI, we show it many examples.

It practices, makes mistakes, and improves—just like learning a new sport or instrument.

Guessing Species...
Monard
Blue Morpho

AI Needs Humans

Emma's robot vacuum bumps into a chair and stops. "*Why won't you move*?" Emma giggles. Her brother says, "*Because someone still has to teach it where to go*!" Emma nods. "So *AI needs humans to guide it*?"

AI doesn't train itself. People create the rules, collect data, fix mistakes, and choose how AI should act.

AI is powerful — but humans stay in charge.

Predictions

Before Emma taps "**play**," her video app suggests the next video she might like. "**How does it know**?" she laughs.

AI makes predictions—smart guesses based on patterns.

It can't see the future, but it can guess what you might like next.

Why AI Makes Mistakes

Emma's camera app mistakes her cat for a raccoon.
"***Rude***!" she says, hugging her cat. "**You're definitely not a raccoon**."

AI is not perfect.
Sometimes it sees patterns wrong and makes silly mistakes.

Humans must help check and correct them.

ERROR!
RACCOON

AI Has Limits

Noah asks his tablet, "*What's my dog thinking right now*?"

The tablet buzzes. "*I... don't know.*"

Emma laughs. "S*ee? AI can't do everything*!"

Noah sighs. "*Not even mind reading*?"

AI is smart in some ways but limited in others. It can detect patterns, read text, or recognize pictures — but it cannot guess feelings, read minds, or know everything.

Teaching a Robot

In club, students build a tiny robot.
It wanders in circles until someone shows it the right path.
"*It needs training*!" Emma says.

Robots use AI to follow rules, learn simple tasks, and respond to the world.

They need clear examples to understand what to do.

Where AI Gets Confused

Emma shows the robot a picture of her cat wrapped in a blanket.
"*Is this a burrito*?" the robot blurts.
Everyone bursts into laughter.
"*No! It's my cat!*" Emma says.

AI can get confused when pictures are tricky or unusual. It uses patterns — if the pattern looks different, it might guess wrong. That's normal learning.

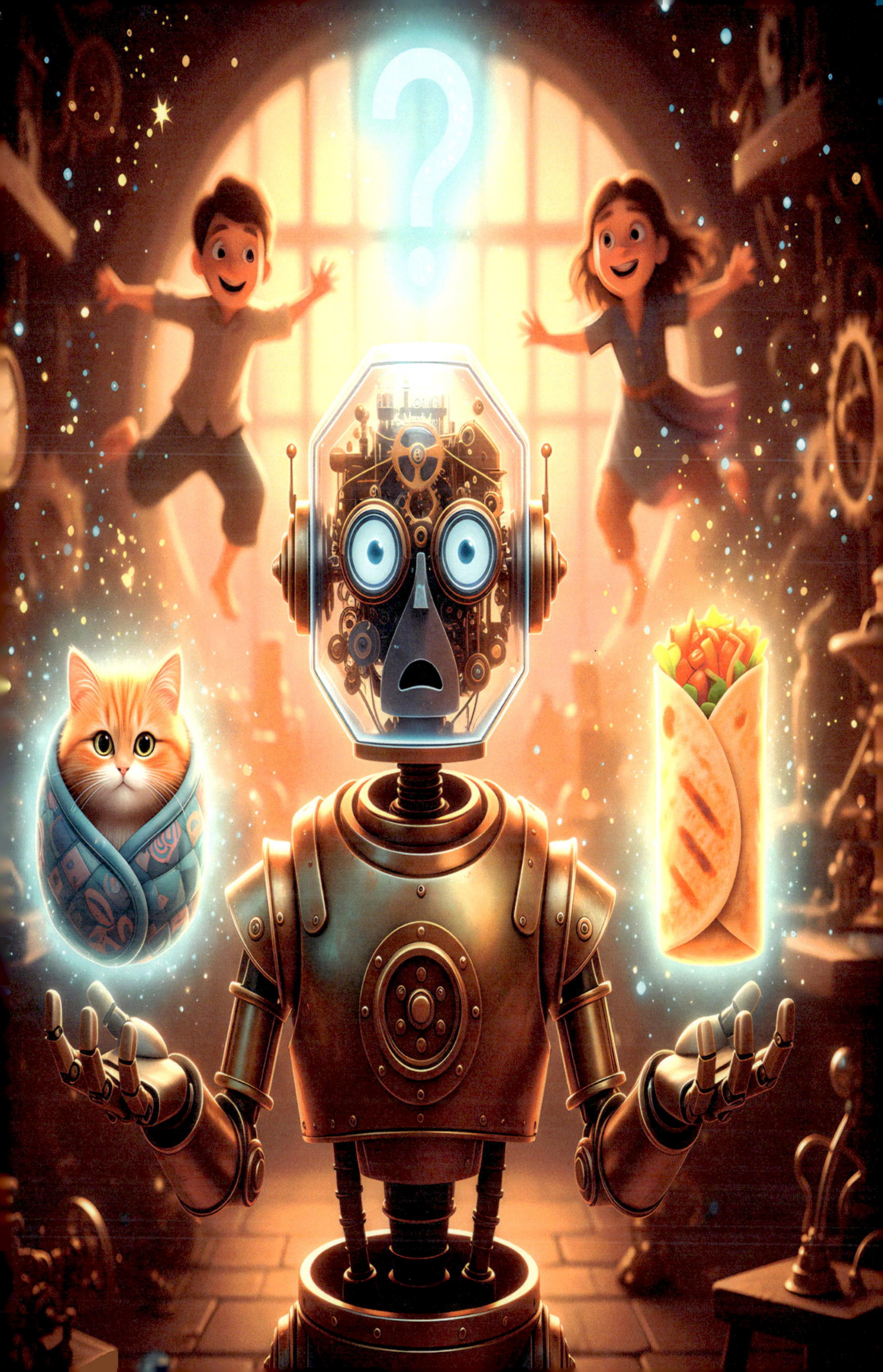

Voice Assistants

Emma tries, "*Hey smart speaker, tell me a joke*!"

The speaker lights up and answers with a silly robot laugh.

AI can listen to words, turn them into meaning, and find helpful responses.

This is called **speech recognition**.

Why did the scarecrow win aword? Because ho outtsnding in the field!
What to u call berty kengraw?
What you "S lazy kangraoo?
Pouch Potato!

AI in Games

When Emma's character pauses in the forest, the game creatures still roam around. "**They're moving on their own,**" she notices.

Games use AI to control characters, make challenges, and respond to players.

AI helps games feel alive and exciting.

Smart Cameras

Emma's camera draws little squares around faces.

"*How does it know where we are*?" she asks.

This is computer vision—AI that helps machines understand what they see using pictures and patterns.

Maps & Directions

During a family trip, their map app warns: "**Traffic ahead!**"

"*Thanks, little AI helper*," Emma says.

Maps use AI to combine traffic data, street speed, and patterns to find the fastest path.

Learning From Mistakes

Emma's drawing app guesses her doodle is a snail—when it's clearly a dragon.
"*It's okay*," she laughs. "*Try again*!"

AI improves when it sees what it got wrong. It learns from mistakes just like 10-year old kids do.

SNAIL

Helping People

Emma visits her grandma, whose tablet reads recipes aloud.
"*It helps me see and hear better*," Grandma says.

AI can assist people—reading text, guiding navigation, translating speech, and helping with daily tasks.

AI Helps Everyone Differently

Emma's grandma visits the school.
She taps her tablet and reads aloud using a speech assistant.
Noah whispers, "*That's AI too*?"
Emma nods proudly.

AI can help different people with different needs:

- Reading text aloud
- Translating languages
- Finding information
- Guiding directions

It supports humans of all ages.

The Future of AI

As Emma falls asleep, she imagines future helpers—robots planting trees, smart tools saving energy, and machines teaming with humans.

AI is growing fast.
The future will bring new inventions, new helpers, and new responsibilities for 10-year-old kids who learn how AI works today.

Robots With Sensors

During robotics club, Noah taps a little robot's head.
Its lights blink as it turns toward her hand.
"*It felt my tap*!" he says.
"*Yep*," Emma replies, "*sensors help it notice the world*."

Robots use sensors—like tiny digital eyes, ears, and touchpads—to understand what's around them.

AI uses this information to decide what to do next.

Image Classification

Noah snaps a picture of a flower.
His app pops up: "*Is this a sunflower*?"
He taps "*Yes*!"
Now the app gets better at recognizing flowers next time.

AI can look at pictures and sort them into groups. This is called image classification—teaching AI to recognize what things are.

PLANT:
SUNFLOWER

Understanding Words

Emma types "*Tell me a fun fact*!"
Her tablet replies with one instantly:
"**Octopuses have three hearts**!"
Emma giggles. "*That's wild*."

AI can read and understand words using natural language processing.

It figures out what you mean so it can answer or help.

Translation Magic

Emma meets a new classmate who speaks another language.
They type into a translator app that shows both languages at once.
"*Cool*!" they say together—even though the words look different.

Some AI tools can translate one language into another.

They match meanings instead of just swapping words.

ADVENTURE!
¡AVENTURA!

Sorting and Grouping

In art class, Emma's tablet groups her doodles into piles: animals, shapes, and plants.
"*I didn't even tell it*!" she says, amazed.

AI can cluster things—grouping similar items even when no labels are given.
It notices what looks alike all by itself.

Try, Learn, Try Again

Emma programs a little digital character to find treasure in a maze.
At first it bumps into walls.
Then slowly… it learns the right path.
"*Go, little explorer*!" she cheers.

This is reinforcement learning—AI learning by trial and error.

It tries something, checks the result, and improves.

TRY AGAIN
AGAIN
TRY AGAIN

Safe and Kind AI

At school, students discuss how AI should behave.
"*Should AI be fair*?"
"*Should it protect privacy*?"
Everyone nods.
"*People decide how to make AI responsible.*"

AI should be built safely and fairly.

Humans create rules and guardrails to keep it helpful, respectful, and kind.

THE
FAIRNESS ADVENTURE
HEARTS, SHIELDS & SCALES

Humans + AI Together

In science fair planning, Emma imagines a future where humans and machines team up—building, learning, even solving big world problems together.
"*AI isn't here to replace u*s," she thinks. "*It's here to help us.*"

The best AI systems work with people.
Humans provide creativity and ideas.

AI provides speed and pattern-finding.
Together, they make powerful teams.

Personalization

When Noah opens his reading app, it shows stories with dragons—his favorite.
"*Did it... remember*?" he wonders, smiling.

Some AI systems learn what you like.
This is called personalization—adjusting choices for each person.

Recommenders

Emma finishes a puzzle game.
Right away, the app says, "*Try this next*!"
She taps it and laughs—it's exactly her style.

Recommendation systems use your past choices to suggest new things—videos, books, songs, or games.

Smart Search

During a science report, Noah types "**animals with superpowers**."
His search tool instantly shows octopuses, frogs, and beetles with surprising abilities.
"*That was fast*!"

AI helps search engines find information quickly by matching your question with billions of results.

superpower animals

Maps That Learn

When Emma bikes to school, her map app warns her about a slippery road ahead. “**How did it know?**” she gasps.

Maps use AI to combine traffic, weather, and past data.

The more data they get, the better they can guide you safely.

AI in Medicine

Emma's aunt works at a clinic.
She shows Emma a screen where AI helps doctors spot tiny details in X-rays.
"*It helps us see things we might miss*," she explains.

AI can support doctors by finding patterns in medical images or records—helping people stay healthy.

AI in Safety

At the park, Emma notices a drone checking for missing pets.
A volunteer says, "A*I helps us scan large areas quickly.*"

AI tools can help find lost pets, predict dangers, or scan areas safely—always supervised by humans.

Human Creativity + AI Tools

Noah draws a castle, and his sketching app suggests styles—sparkly, medieval, futuristic.
He picks one and adds his own twist.
"*It's helping me imagine more*!"

AI tools don't replace creativity—they expand it.
Humans bring ideas.
AI offers new possibilities.

AI + Imagination

At art club, Emma draws a castle and asks her tablet for ideas.
It shows glowing versions: futuristic, rainbow, underwater.
"*Wow*!" she says. "*AI helps my imagination grow*!"

AI cannot imagine on its own — but it can help humans explore ideas.

Humans bring creativity.
AI brings possibilities.

The 10-year old kid Who Knows AI

At the school showcase, Emma explains AI to younger classes.
She teaches them about patterns, data, and robots.
"*You already know so much*!" her teacher says proudly.

When 10-year-old kids learn how AI works, they gain skills for the future.

Understanding AI helps them become builders, thinkers, and problem-solvers.

Ai

★ ASSESSMENT PACK OVERVIEW

1. **Exam A — Basic Check (10 Questions)**
2. **Exam B — Standard Test (15 Questions)**
3. **Exam C — Challenge Test (20 Questions)**
4. **Short-Answer Section**
5. **Performance Task (project-style assessment)**
6. **Answer Key**
7. **Rubrics** (3 types: multiple-choice, short answer, performance task)

■ EXAM A — BASIC CHECK (10 Questions)

Multiple Choice

AI stands for:
a) Animal Intelligence
b) Artificial Intelligence
c) Awesome Ideas

AI learns by studying:
a) Patterns
b) Magic
c) Random guesses

Data is:
a) Information
b) Toys
c) Food

Which device often uses AI?
a) A rock
b) A smart speaker
c) A pencil

Which device often uses AI?

a) A rock

b) A smart speaker

c) A pencil

AI sometimes makes:

a) Perfect choices

b) No choices

c) Mistakes

True or False

AI can learn from examples.

Robots use sensors to understand the world.

AI can see pictures using computer vision.

AI replaces humans completely.

Maps can use AI to find faster routes.

■ EXAM B — STANDARD TEST (15 Questions)

(Good for ages 8–11)

Multiple Choice

AI uses patterns to:
a) Decorate the screen
b) Make smart guesses
c) Play music automatically

Training AI means:
a) Teaching it with many examples
b) Making it run laps
c) Turning it on and off

A prediction is:
a) A guess based on patterns
b) A secret message
c) A type of robot

Computer vision helps AI:
a) Smell food
b) See images
c) Cut paper

Natural Language Processing helps AI:
a) Speak and understand words
b) Build houses
c) Grow plants

Short Answer
What is data?
Why can AI make mistakes?
How does reinforcement learning help AI improve?
Give one example of AI in everyday life.
Why do robots use sensors?

True or False

AI can translate languages.

AI always gets things right.

Kids can learn how AI works.

AI uses examples to learn.

AI helps people in many ways.

■ EXAM C — CHALLENGE TEST (20 Questions)

(Great for upper grades or enrichment groups)

Multiple Choice

AI improves when it:
a) Ignores mistakes
b) Learns from errors
c) Stops learning

Data can be:
a) Pictures, numbers, or words
b) Only numbers
c) Only drawings

Which of these is an example of computer vision?
a) A camera recognizing a face
b) A speaker playing music
c) A timer ringing

Sensors help robots:
a) Guess
b) Understand their surroundings
c) Read books

One example of reinforcement learning is:
a) A robot trying different paths until it finds the right one
b) A robot reading a story
c) A robot standing still

Short Answer
Explain what a "pattern" is.
Describe one way AI helps people.
How does AI learn from examples?
What is computer vision?
What is Natural Language Processing?

True or False

AI can work with humans as a team.

AI learns instantly with no practice needed.

Maps sometimes use AI to detect traffic.

Robots only need one sensor to understand everything.

AI is used in medicine to find patterns in images.

Personalized apps use AI to suggest things you might like.

AI is a tool humans create.

■ SHORT ANSWER SECTION (Use with any exam)

In your own words, what is AI?
Why does AI need data?
What is one mistake AI can make?
How does a robot "sense" the world?
Explain how AI recognizes a picture or word.

■ PERFORMANCE TASK (Project Assessment)

(Excellent for teachers/homeschoolers)

Task:
Design Your Own AI Helper
Create a drawing and a short explanation for an AI tool that could help someone at home, school, or in the community.

Include:
What the AI helper does
What data it learns from
One mistake it might make
How it improves over time
Students may draw their tool, label its sensors, and write a short paragraph.

ANSWER KEY

Exam A

1. b
2. a
3. a
4. b
5. c
6. True
7. True
8. True
9. False
10. True

Exam B

1. b
2. a
3. a
4. b
5. a
6. Data is information.
7. AI makes mistakes because it doesn't understand perfectly or has limited examples.
8. It improves by trying, failing, and trying again.
9. Answers vary: smart speaker, maps, games, camera, etc.
10. Sensors help robots detect surroundings.
11. True
12. False
13. True
14. True
15. True

Exam C

1. b
2. a
3. a
4. b
5. a
6. 6–13. Open responses (rubric below)
7. True
8. False
9. True
10. False
11. True
12. True
13. True

■ RUBRICS

★ Multiple-Choice / True–False Rubric (Auto-graded)

- Correct answer: 1 point
- Incorrect answer: 0 points

Score categories:

- Excellent: 90–100%
- Strong Understanding: 75–89%
- Developing: 50–74%
- Needs Support: Below 50%

★ Short-Answer Rubric (0–3 points each)

Description

Score

3 Clear, correct explanation using kid-friendly reasoning; gives example if needed

2 Mostly correct; missing detail or clarity

1 Partially correct; shows confusion

0 Incorrect or no response

⭐ Performance Task Rubric (0–4 points per category)

Total Score: 16 points

Category	4	3	2	1
Creativity	Unique, thoughtful AI tool	Clear idea	Simple idea	Little effort
Understanding AI	Shows strong understanding	Mostly correct	Some errors	Incorrect
Use of Data Patterns	Explains data clearly	Mentions data	Minimal mention	No mention
Description & Clarity	Well-written, clear	Mostly clear	Some confusion	Incomplete

GLOSSARY

Artificial Intelligence (AI):
A computer system that can learn simple patterns and make decisions.

Data:
Information—pictures, numbers, words, sounds—that helps AI learn.

Patterns:
Things that happen again and again.

Machine Learning:
Teaching AI with lots of examples so it can improve over time.

Prediction:
A smart guess based on past patterns.

Sensors:
Tools that help robots see, hear, or feel the world.

Computer Vision:
AI that helps machines understand pictures.

Natural Language Processing:
AI that helps machines understand words and sentences.

Reinforcement Learning:
AI that learns by trying, making mistakes, and trying again.

■ THINK & TALK QUESTIONS

Perfect for teachers, parents, and classroom discussions.

1. Where do you see AI in your everyday life?
2. What is one way AI helps people?
3. Why do you think AI sometimes makes mistakes?
4. If you could teach a robot anything, what would it be?
5. What kind of AI tool would you invent for the future?

■ ACTIVITY PAGE

Draw Your Own AI Helper!

Imagine a friendly AI tool that could help you at home or school.

What would it look like?

What could it do?

Give it a name!

■ ABOUT THE SERIES

AI for Beginners — *Kids Edition* is an 8-book learning path designed to introduce **Artificial Intelligence** in a fun, simple, story-driven way.

Book 1 — Introduction to AI
Book 2 — Symbolic AI
Book 3 — Neural Networks
Book 4 — Computer Vision
Book 5 — Natural Language AI
Book 6 — Other AI Techniques
Book 7 — AI Ethics
Book 8 — Mega Activity Book

Each book builds on the last, helping kids grow confident with STEM concepts one step at a time.

■ ABOUT AI CIRCUIT

AI Circuit creates engaging, age-friendly books that help kids explore the exciting world of Artificial Intelligence, robotics, and modern **STEM** learning.

Our books are designed to:

- Make complex ideas easy to understand
- Spark curiosity
- Encourage creative problem-solving
- Build confidence with future-ready skills

Learn more, explore activities, and discover new books at: **Amazon.com**

■ COMING NEXT...

Book 2: Symbolic AI
Learn how robots follow rules, use logic, and make step-by-step decisions!

A friendly look at "If–Then" thinking, simple reasoning, and how early AI systems worked. Stay tuned!

Thank you for reading and learning with us!

If this book helped make Artificial Intelligence easier or more exciting for a young reader, we'd be incredibly grateful if you left a **quick review on Amazon**.

Reviews help us continue our work—researching Artificial Intelligence and explaining it in a way that is **accurate, informative, and kid-friendly**.

We're grateful for your support.

Made in the USA
Las Vegas, NV
03 November 2026

57422081R00119